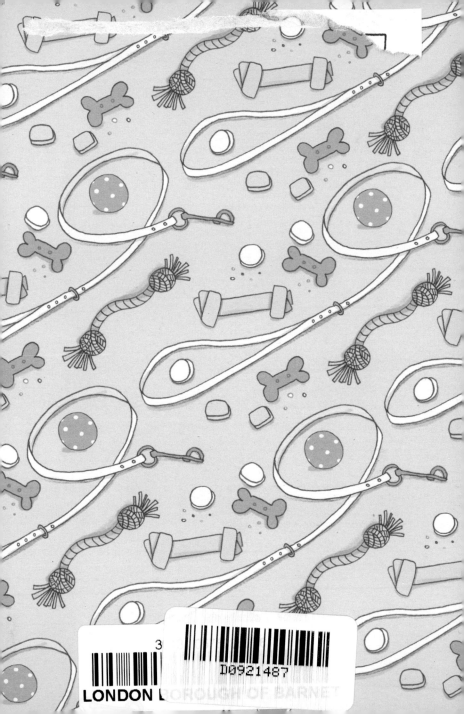

DOGS

Understanding your very
BEST FRIEND

Expert advice from
DR JOHN BRADSHAW

Illustrated by Clare Elsom

ANDERSEN PRESS

First published in 2021 by
Andersen Press Limited
20 Vauxhall Bridge Road
London SW1V 2SA

Vijverlaan 48,
3062 HL Rotterdam, Nederland
www.andersenpress.co.uk

2 4 6 8 10 9 7 5 3 1

British Library Cataloguing in Publication Data available.

ISBN 978 1 83913 087 8

Printed and bound in in Great Britain by Clays Ltd, Elcograf S.p.A.

To all dogs everywhere,
but especially Alexis, Ivan, Bruno and Ginger,
for sharing their secrets.

Hello!

I'm Dr John Bradshaw.

I'm a biologist, but unlike most biologists
I study pets, dogs and cats in particular. In
this book I am going to let you into the secret
of how dogs experience the world, and what
they think about it. This book will help you
to be the best friend you can be to your dog.
To let you into this secret, my good friend
Rusty has agreed to let us follow
him around for a day.

Rusty

Meet **Rusty Barker**. He's a terrier, a kind of dog whose original purpose was to keep rats away from farms and houses. These days most terriers are just household pets, but they still know how to sniff out a rat!

Of course, Rusty's not his *real* name, because he's a dog. When dogs are talking to each other, they use smell-names, not sound-names. But he knows that when humans say 'Rusty', that means *him*, so that's what he answers to.

Smells, smells, smells

What's it like being a dog like Rusty? It's not like being a grown-up. It's not like being a child. It's not like being an alien, either.

grown-up

child

alien

dog

Dogs are like us in a lot of ways. They can see, hear and feel most things that we can. But they also have a superpower: their sense of smell. That's why they sniff things all the time.

Most animals live somewhere in the World of Smells.

You and I live in the World, which is everything we can see. Dogs, cats, mice, snakes, ants, moths and lots of other animals mostly live in the World of Smells, which is the same World as ours, but much, *much* stinkier.

Super nose

It's full of poo smells,

pee smells,

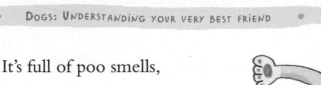

leaf smells,

sweaty foot smells

and loads of other stinks that we don't even have names for, because our noses aren't as smart as theirs.

The first thing humans notice is usually what things look like. But dogs mostly care about what things smell like. That's why you like watching TV and YouTube, and dogs don't. YouTube for dogs would have to literally be a tube with stinky smells coming out of it all the time.

Yuck, you're thinking. That would mean that YouTube for dogs would make your house stink like a gigantic fart. But actually, it wouldn't have to, because dogs' noses are so sensitive that they'd only need a tiny amount of each smell, such a small amount that you wouldn't even know it was there.

A dog's eyesight isn't as good as yours, and they couldn't care less if something is pink or blue, just so long as it smells interesting. That's why the pictures in this book are in black and white, because that's roughly how dogs see things. Smells are their colours. Their sense of smell isn't magic, it's just a way of experiencing the world differently to you.

Put it another way: just because you can't see something doesn't mean it doesn't exist.

You know how to use the TV remote, don't you? (OK, probably better than your parents do.) You can't actually *see* the remote talking to the TV, but it must do, because the TV does what the remote tells it to do. The remote talks to the TV using infra-red light, a kind of light that your eyes can't see.

Well, that's a bit like how smells are for dogs. There are loads of smells that dogs find really exciting, but we have no clue about, because they are just too weak for our noses.

Early morning

When Rusty wakes up in the morning, he sniffs the air before he even opens his eyes. His nose tells him that no one has come downstairs yet, because none of the people smells have changed from last night. It's not walkies time yet!

A few moments later, Mum comes downstairs in her dressing gown and opens the door to the garden. Out goes Rusty. He's desperate for a pee, but first he has to have a sniff around the garden to discover what's happened out there while he's been asleep.

Right away, he arrives at a place where he can smell that a cat has been walking across the lawn during the night. There's nothing to see, no dents in the grass or yucky furballs, but Rusty's nose lets him trace every pawprint that the cat made, just from the little bit of cat foot smell left behind (which I guess to a dog, is much sweeter-smelling than human foot smell. Let's blame socks. And don't even mention welly boots. Sorry, back to cats).

Rusty can even tell which way the cat was moving, just from the differences between the smells of her pawprints. The fresher they are, the stronger the scent, so the direction she's gone in is smellier than the direction she came from.

The World of Smells is always changing.

Mice have been scuttling about during the night, marking their trails with little spots of pee.

A twig sits on the lawn, a sappy smell coming from where a clumsy pigeon broke it off from the tree above.

There's the smell of cut grass in the corner from when Dad mowed the lawn yesterday.

A sweet wrapper that just blew in from the street pongs of mint.

Next time you're in a garden, try crawling around with your nose to the ground, sniffing as you go. That way you'll get a bit of an idea of what it's like to be a dog, although your human nose won't give you much of the detail.

It would be like always being
close to something really
smelly – a vase of flowers,

chocolate brownies
straight from the oven,

a really bad fart (fingers
crossed it's brownies!).

And all these smells alter with the wind
and the weather, which means they change
and shift all the time. This makes for a very
exciting morning for Rusty.

He can tell
straight away that it rained the
night before, and not just because
his paws are wet, but because there are even
more interesting smells around than usual.
Rain washes old smells out of the ground
and plants' leaves, reminding Rusty of things
that happened a few days ago.

That's a bit like when your mum and
her friends flick through loads of photos
on their phones when they meet up. Except
that dogs don't need to take pictures, because
they remember everything their
noses tell them!

nares

You can see how important smells are to dogs just by looking at their nostrils, where the air goes in and out. Yours point downwards. Maybe this is to keep the rain out, but it also means your nostrils can't be pushed up against things to get all the details of the smell. Not unless you want people staring at you.

Anyway, most of the time you keep yours way up in the air, which is not the best way to capture all the lovely pongs near the ground. Dogs can lower their heads right down to the ground, and their nostrils point forwards so that they can sniff what's right in front of them. (Dogs' nostrils are called 'nares', which rhymes with 'fairies').

But it's the *inside* of their noses where dogs are so much better equipped than we are. The air that they sniff into their nostrils swirls through a special 3D maze made of bones called 'turbinates'. If you could lay the maze out flat, it would be roughly the size of two smartphone screens. That's an amazing amount of surface to cram into a small head.

The walls of the maze are covered with

eight hundred different kinds of smell
detectors. Smell detectors are microscopic
hairs that stick out of the surface of the
nostril-maze and catch the smells as they go
by. If it's the kind of smell that matches that
kind of detector, the other end of the hair
sends a message to the brain ('roses', 'poo',
'newly mown grass' or 'garlic' – and lots of
others).

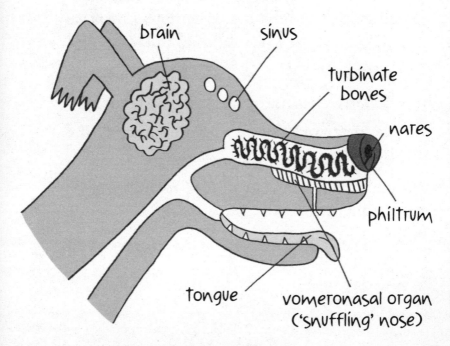

brain

sinus

turbinate
bones

nares

philtrum

tongue

vomeronasal organ
('snuffling' nose)

We actually have the same detectors that dogs do, but only a few hundred of each. Dogs have about a *million* of each kind, and almost a billion altogether. That's why they're so much better at smelling than we are.

Someone new

Back to our trusty Rusty. Rusty trots round the garden, taking in all the lovely smells. Then he has a quick pee and heads back indoors, where all of his humans are rushing around, getting ready for school and work. There's Mum, Dad, Bella (who's ten) and Ned (who's eight).

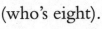

Rusty is used to all of the commotion, but right now he's concentrating on an appetising smell that's coming from Ned's school bag. Ned has forgotten that there's a half-eaten cheese sandwich wedged into one of the pockets on the outside. He and Rusty get to the bag at just the same moment. As Ned tries to load up his school books, he finds Rusty's head in his way. Ned looks round quickly to make sure Mum and Dad aren't watching, and then helps Rusty get at the sandwich.

It's a bit crispy, and covered in fluff from the bag, but Rusty doesn't care! He trots off to his bed and munches it down.

Outside, there's the sound of a car parking, and someone is greeted at the front door. Rusty rushes to say hello. Then he stops for a moment. This is someone he's never met before, a new friend of Ned's who's getting a lift to school from Mum. Mum can see he's a bit nervous of Rusty, so she squats down to his level and shows him how to say hello to Rusty. She tells him that he can pat Rusty on the back if he likes, but first he should turn sideways so Rusty doesn't think he's being stared at (some dogs hate that) and hold out a fist for Rusty to sniff. Carefully, Rusty goes up to him to find out more about him.

And naturally, this means he needs to catch his smell. You or I recognise someone mainly by what their face looks like, but dogs recognise people from their smells.

Rusty goes up to the stranger and sniffs, and although no one notices, that's not all he does. Dogs have a secret way of smelling people that most humans don't know anything about. In their World of Smells, dogs don't just rely on their noses. When they get close to a person (or another dog) they don't know, they try to snuffle them.

Snuffling is where they lick someone's hand and then use their tongues to push the lick up into the top of their mouths. Here, they have a special other nose that humans don't have. Dogs can remember the snuffles of hundreds of people and dogs, just like you can remember lots of people's faces. Next time he meets Ned's friend, he'll remember him by his snuffle as well as his smell.

Walkies

Soon, everyone apart from Dad has left the house. When Dad picks up Rusty's lead, Rusty gets super excited. He knows that it's time for his walk in the park!

Rusty loves his walks, because they are the smelliest part of his day. All the way to the park he pulls this way and that on his lead, annoying Dad, who's on his phone, trying to catch up on some work.

Rusty can smell the pee-marks left by other dogs on every lamp-post they pass, and of course he has to lift his leg on each one to leave a little pee of his own – 'I woz 'ere!'

Dogs find out what's going on by sniffing everything and everyone they meet. That means you, and all the other humans they meet, and all the other animals they meet, and all the tree trunks they meet, and all the patches of grass they run across, and all the sticks they pick up, and, of course, all kinds of poo, everywhere – bird poo, dog poo, badger poo, fox poo and mouse poo.

Dogs like to sniff around everywhere they go, and especially when they go for a walk. That's how they find out about what's happening with all the other dogs in the neighbourhood. It's also why they like to take their time when they sniff a lamp-post.

And it's why boy dogs like to pee on every bush and tuft of grass and post that they pass. They want to let all the other dogs know they've been out and about.

(Girl dogs are often a bit more careful about where they pee. They don't like to draw attention to themselves, in case a rough boy dog decides to chase after them.)

Just as Rusty gets to the park, another dog comes round the corner. He must have hurt his paw, because he's wearing a bandage and hopping on three legs. When he gets to the park gates, and tries to lift his back leg to pee, he falls over!

Dad lets Rusty off his lead, and Rusty rushes off to look for the most thrilling smell he can find. Today, Rusty thinks he's caught a whiff of a fox's pawprint on the ground.

Superpower sniffing

Dogs have a trick that helps them get the most out of every smell they come across. When they're sniffing, dogs change the way they breathe. Rusty's doing it now, as he tries to work out which way the fox has gone. To us, it sounds a bit like panting, but dogs don't do it because they're out of breath, they do it when they are trying to get every last detail of a particularly exciting smell.

First, dogs sniff in a little bit of air through the big hole at the front of each nostril, and send it deep into their heads, into the place where all the smells get sorted out. Then they do a little snort out through the slits at the side of each nostril, wrinkling the skin so that the air doesn't go straight out but downwards, past their mouths. This pulls more air over the place where the smell is coming from, so more of it comes in at the next sniff. Clever, eh? Bet you can't do that with your nose!

First

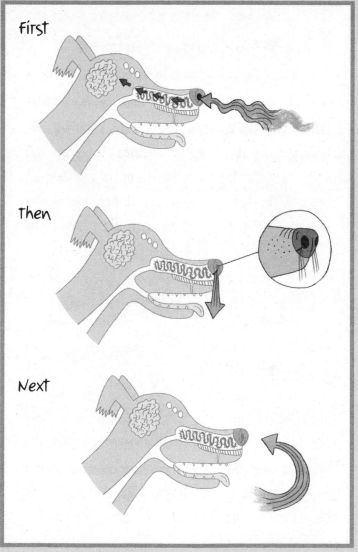

Then

Next

31

Even though their noses are very sensitive, some dogs love really strong pongs as well, like fox poo or bags of rotting rubbish. Sometimes when Rusty finds something really stinky, he decides to roll in it, even though he has to have a bath when he gets home, and Rusty doesn't like baths.

No one really knows why dogs like stinky things so much. Perhaps it's a bit like dressing up. You like to dress up as a pirate or a princess or a robot sometimes, don't you? Perhaps dogs are just the same, except they like to try out really niffy pongs.

Rusty has been thinking so much about fox smells that now he's lost sight of Dad. He's run so far that he hasn't noticed that Dad stopped a couple of minutes ago to answer his phone. Now, he's so worried about losing Dad that he forgets all about the fox.

You or I will call out someone's name if we can't see them, but dogs find people by their smell. Which is very useful, because they can't manage a different bark for everyone they know!

Smells can be hard to track down. When you can see something, you immediately know where it is, but smells aren't like that. They often don't travel in straight lines. They are carried around on the wind, and winds can wiggle all over the place. These wiggles are called 'eddies', and although you can't see

them in the air, you can see something similar in water, perhaps when you're standing on a bridge looking down at a stream. After it goes past a rock, the water spins around for a while, even as it carries on moving downstream. The same thing happens with air.

Luckily, today the wind is blowing Dad's smell towards Rusty. When dogs come across a smell and can't tell where it's come from, they start by running just a little way towards where the wind is coming from. Then, they slow down for a moment and sniff again. If the smell is still there, they'll run a bit further in the same direction. But if it seems to have disappeared, they'll turn left or right and then zigzag this way and that, keeping the wind on the side of their noses. That's why dogs keep their noses wet by licking them —

the side where the wind's coming from feels colder. (Try licking all round the top of your finger, and then blowing on one side to feel how it works!) Then, when they think they've found the smell, they start running towards the wind again.

Rusty soon catches sight of someone who looks like Dad and runs straight to him. But when he gets there and gives him a quick snuffle, he realises it isn't Dad at all! Oops! Luckily, Dad is not far away and calls Rusty over so they can carry on with their walk.

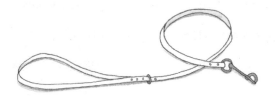

Meeting other dogs

Now Rusty has seen his friend Bruno coming into the park.

Smells are very important to dogs, but so too are their friends. Dog-friends are special because dogs can talk to each other by wagging their tails and moving their ears around – and they can tell a lot about how other dogs are feeling by the way they smell.

Most dogs are happy to meet other dogs. When humans meet, they sometimes hug, or shake each others' hands, but often they just keep apart and say things like 'Hello' or 'How are you?'. That would never do for a dog. Dogs get to know one another by sniffing. They don't always remember faces, but they do remember a smell. That's why dogs always sniff each other when they meet, especially around their bottoms, which is where the best smells are to be found. Or at least they try to. Some dogs are shy and want to get away before the other dog has finished sniffing.

Dogs prefer to check out other dogs by their smell, rather than by what they look like. If it's a dog they don't know, it's so they can remember them for next time. And if it's a dog they've met before, it's to check that they still smell the same. That's because all dogs' smells change a little, every day. Maybe one has just been given a bath, and he smells of flowery shampoo (nice for us, but probably yucky for a dog!). Maybe he's been having fun rolling in something smelly, and his humans haven't noticed yet. And even without a bath, dogs' smells gradually change all by themselves. If two dogs haven't met one another for a while, both their smells will be a little bit different to the last time, because every meal they have affects their smell a tiny bit. When Bruno sniffs Rusty's head, he can even smell the cheese sandwich that Rusty sneaked from Ned's school bag.

Imagine if your dad grew a beard while he was away for a few days. You might not recognise him at first when he got home, until he said hello – his voice hasn't changed! Then you'd run up to him and give him a big hug.

In the olden days, when it was OK for them to roam about during the day, dogs needed to know all about the other dogs

39

in the neighbourhood. Which dogs were mean, which ones were laid-back, which dogs would share a scrap of food that they'd found, and which ones would fight if anyone got in their way.

Nowadays, getting to know every dog doesn't matter so much, but dogs haven't worked that out yet. They still want to try, which is why they pee on lamp-posts and sniff other dogs' bottoms.

Out in the park, Rusty is always on the lookout for other dogs to play with. Best of all, he likes dogs his own size. Big dogs can be a bit clumsy when they play, though they're usually good-tempered. Tiny dogs can be a bit snappy, perhaps because they worry about getting knocked over or trodden on.

Some kinds of dog, like greyhounds and sheepdogs, can be a bit nervous, and so Rusty is careful not to upset them when he's asking them to play.

Tails tell tales

To show other dogs that he's friendly, Rusty always wags his tail from side to side. If he's really excited, or perhaps because he recognises the other dog as a friend, like Bruno, his tail will go really fast. But a wagging tail doesn't always mean that a dog is happy. If he's scared, Rusty sometimes tucks his tail down between his legs and wags it very quickly. And he's learned that a dog whose tail is stiff and sticking up, even though it's wagging a bit, is saying 'I don't like you, don't come any closer'. (It's really important that children like you understand this too, so that you don't get bitten by mistake.)

Friendly   Scared   Don't come any closer

Rusty doesn't like it when dogs stare at him, because it often means that they don't like him. (So it's best not to stare at a dog you don't know, in case it thinks you're angry with it.)

Dogs who don't want to be sniffed may hold their tails up and growl. Others will look away and try to hide behind their human's legs. Either way, Rusty knows that it's best to leave those dogs alone.

Most dogs do like playing, though. Rusty can show that he wants to play by doing a little bow, like this:

This is special dog language for 'Please play with me'. Very smart humans know this, and get down on all fours and push their arms out in front when they want to play. Dogs love that!

If he's playing with a dog he trusts, like his old friend Bruno, Rusty will roll on his back and allow the other dog to pretend to attack him. To make the game more fun, he may even make a noise a bit like a short, high-pitched growl, but he's careful not to growl for real, otherwise the other dog might get scared and run away, or even bite him. He's also careful to keep his mouth slightly open and loose, so the other dog can see he's not ready to bite – which is what would happen if the fight was for real, not a game.

Some dogs like chasing games, especially if Rusty takes turns at being the chaser, otherwise it gets boring. In fact, whatever the game, taking turns is really important for dogs, just like it is for kids!

Most dogs like to play tugging games, but not all of them play fair. If they try to grab a stick that Rusty is carrying, he's learned that they may not be playing fairly. Some try to pull his stick away from him and run off with it. Rusty doesn't usually mind too much if that happens, because he

knows he can always find another stick, but some dogs get cross when their stick is taken, because they think that the stick is *theirs*. So Rusty's always a bit careful when he's playing at tug with another dog, unless it's Bruno, who's always good at sharing.

Given the choice, Rusty would rather play tug with a human, maybe with a bit of rope or a special toy. He's learned that humans don't really want to take the rope or the toy away, what they want is to have fun playing. It's the same with balls. He knows that the only reason that humans want dogs to bring a ball back is so they can throw it again.

When Dad remembers (though today he's forgotten!) he brings a ball to the park to play with Rusty. He knows that although

lots of people think it's OK to pick up and throw any old stick for their dog, that's not actually a great idea, because sometimes sticks can break into sharp pieces and hurt a dog's mouth. Even worse, dogs can sometimes get a piece of stick stuck in their throat and have to be rushed to the animal hospital to have it taken out. So, it's a good thing that Bruno's got his ball, and that Rusty and Bruno know each other well enough to share it.

Doggy dreams

When Rusty and Bruno finish their game, Rusty is happy for Dad to put him back on the lead and head for home. He knows that after walk time, it's lunchtime! Anyway, he's tired from all that sniffing, just as you are after a long morning at school. First, he needs a snack, so Dad shakes some biscuits into his bowl and Rusty wuffles them down. Then he heads for his bed to take a nap. But just before he falls asleep, he gives his paws a sniff, which reminds him of all the fun he had on his walk.

Rusty falls asleep and soon he's rolled over on his back and is snoring contentedly. After a while he stops snoring and starts making tiny little barking noises, and his paws begin to twitch. He's having a dream, and judging by how excited his little barks are getting, the dream could be about chasing squirrels (although in real life they always get away).

Because their noses are so important to them, dogs must also dream about lovely smells: perhaps their favourite food, or the smells of their best friends that they meet in the park.

Just like people, dogs need to dream so their brains can tidy up everything they've learned that day. That could just be memorising the smells of all the dogs they've met, but it's especially important if they've been to a training class and learned a new command.

Sweet dreams, Rusty!

Remembering

Rusty is woken by Dad hopping through the kitchen on one leg and muttering something rather rude under his breath. He's just realised that there's something stinky sticking to the sole of one of his shoes. Rusty can tell instantly that it's poo, and not just any old poo. It smells rather like super-deluxe cat food, so it's likely to have come from next door's posh cat. Dad stumbles out through the back door and Rusty can hear him scrubbing away at his shoe while balancing on one leg.

Then, Rusty catches a whiff of the disinfectant that Dad is using to clean his shoe, and immediately his mind fills with memories of his life before he came to live where he is now. He hates the smell of disinfectant, not just because it's not very pleasant, but because it reminds him of the time long ago when he didn't belong to anyone, and had to live in a rescue centre with lots of other dogs.

Some of those dogs were pets, like Rusty, who were just hoping for a new home. But some were stray dogs who didn't trust humans, and tried to run away whenever they could.

When they are puppies, dogs desperately want to learn how to love people, but some never get the chance. In fact all over the world there are millions of dogs who have never had a proper owner, and live as best they can, helping themselves to food that's been thrown away, or scraps left out by people who feel sorry for them.

Stray dogs can feel trapped when they are kept in a kennel. They want to get back to the life they know, roaming the streets, even though that is often dangerous and they can get sick from eating rubbish.

Now he's been reminded of it by the smell of the disinfectant, Rusty can remember some of the nervous dogs at the rescue centre, and how the staff tried to make them happier and more confident. Rusty would do almost anything to get a friendly pat, so he was really puzzled when he saw that the dog in the next kennel to him was really scared of being touched at all. One minute, she'd be having a happy sniff-chat with Rusty through the bars of the kennel,

the next, she'd be crouched in the corner with her tail between her legs, shaking all over. The reason? One of the rescue centre staff had just walked past. They hadn't come into her kennel or anything like that, just passed by along the corridor. If anyone did come into her kennel, she'd try to climb the walls just to get away. If someone managed to get a collar and lead on her, she'd eventually calm down a bit, but used to snap as soon as anyone stretched a hand out to her. Rusty got a bit jealous of that bit: he longed for someone to give him a hug and tickle him between his ears.

So for a dog to have a good life and live with a family, it's important that they are treated right when they are puppies. Dogs that haven't got to know people before they are three months old, or have been badly treated when they are young, find it very difficult to trust humans, even though they understand that if humans didn't help them at least a bit, they wouldn't be able to survive at all. If dogs like this do end up being pets, they can be very anxious most of the time.

Some people who have never had a dog before may not know how distressed puppies can be if they haven't been brought up in a happy household.

The rescue centre staff used a clever trick to stop the scared dog being frightened of hands. Most dogs that have had hard lives have been desperately hungry from time to time, so will forget being nervous for a moment if they think that they're about to get something to eat. A hand on its own may be scary (might hit me!) but a hand holding a little piece of yummy cheese is a snack (the cheese, not the hand – but people doing this kind of training wear strong gloves just in case the dog decides to nip them).

Soon, Rusty's new dog-friend learned that hands could be good, not bad, because sometimes hands hold food. Then, she found that the trainer had changed the rules slightly, so that the food disappeared if she rushed in and tried to grab it, and she was only given it if she took it calmly and slowly. In the next stage, the trainer let the scared dog take food from her left hand but only after the dog rubbed her cheek against the trainer's right hand. Soon, the dog came to realise that touching a human was nothing to be scared of, and before long she was jumping into the trainer's lap for a cuddle!

Now, Rusty hears Dad coming back into the house, and as the smell of disinfectant disappears, he gradually forgets all about his time at the rescue centre. Unless something reminds them, dogs don't think much about what happened yesterday, or what's going to happen tomorrow. They're much too busy just being dogs. Dogs with kind owners don't need to worry, because they trust their humans to plan their lives for them.

Sometimes dogs get caught out by not being able to disentangle the present from the past. When Rusty first came to live with Mum and Dad and Bella and Ned (who was just a baby then), they already had an older dog living with them called Poppy. Even now Rusty occasionally comes across tiny scraps of her smell, especially under the stairs where she used to have her bed.

Rusty never really understood what happened to her. One day she seemed sleepy and didn't want to play, and the next day she was simply not there any more. But whenever he's reminded of Poppy by her smell, he also remembers that Mum and Dad were very sad when she left (Bella and Ned were too young to understand).

For a while after that, her smell was everywhere, and sometimes it seemed so fresh that Rusty would run out into the garden looking for her. But she was never there, and after a while he got used to her not being around. Now he only remembers her when he sniffs under the stairs.

Dogs forget the past really quickly, unless something comes along and reminds them.

If Rusty does something he knows Mum and Dad won't like, such as sleep on the sofa when no one's looking, he does feel bad for a couple of minutes, but that doesn't last. A few moments after he's jumped off the sofa, Rusty won't remember that he had been there recently. Luckily, Mum knows that there's no point in telling Rusty he's been a bad dog when she finds hairs on the sofa half an hour after he got off it, because he just won't understand. It's impossible to explain to a dog what he's done wrong, unless he's been caught in the act. I bet you sometimes wish that worked for children, too!

Home alone

Now it's the middle of the afternoon, and Dad has to go out for an hour or so before he picks Ned and Bella up from school. He lets Rusty out into the garden for a few minutes, and then calls him back indoors. He puts on his coat and picks up his car keys from the tray in the hallway. 'Bye, Rusty,' he says. 'Be good!' and disappears through the front door.

Rusty used to get really upset as soon as the last person had left the house, and even now he feels a little bit sad, just for a moment.

When Rusty was a puppy, in his first home, he used to chew things when he was left alone, because he found that helped him forget about being lonely and bored.

Often when his old owner got home he'd shout and give Rusty a smack. Rusty never did work out why, though. After a while he used to dread his old owner coming home. Then one day he took Rusty to the rescue centre and left him there, saying he was 'too destructive'.

Dogs can get very miserable when they're left on their own for long, even when they're at home. Some panic as soon as everyone goes out, barking and whining and running from window to window, trying to work out where their family has disappeared to.

Some dogs get so upset when they're left alone that they are sick all over the floor. Some are so scared, they can't stop themselves peeing in the house, even though they know they're not supposed to. Other dogs chew the corner of the sofa because they find it takes their mind off being lonely.

When Rusty was living in his first home, his owners talked a lot about 'discipline', which seemed to be mainly shouting at him for reasons he couldn't understand.

He got confused, because sometimes they'd shout at him while he was in the middle of doing something wrong, and sometimes for something he'd done an hour ago and, being a dog, had completely forgotten about. And sometimes they just shouted at each other, and even that made Rusty miserable because he thought they might possibly be shouting at him.

They also used to call him 'spiteful' when they found he'd done something wrong, like when he chewed on a slipper (well, he was only a puppy). Rusty didn't understand that they thought he'd chewed the slipper on purpose, just to make them cross. This is way beyond what dogs can understand. It might seem like this is an excuse for the dog, but it's not.

That guilty look

Once upon a time a vet got a phone call from a lady who had a dog called Nick. Whenever she went out, Nick used to pull down the toilet roll and run around the house, chewing it into little pieces. What a mess! Nick's owner firmly believed that Nick was doing this on purpose, just to make her cross, and she especially believed this because every time she came home to find shredded toilet paper all over the place, Nick looked upset. She called that his 'guilty look'.

Does that sound like something dogs can do? Not shredding paper, of course, because what could be more fun than that! No, being able to work out that an owner thinks that shredding toilet paper is a bad thing to do. The vet in this case knew that was beyond a dog's mind.

To prove this, the vet did a simple trick. He went to the owner's house, and he shredded a load of toilet paper and left it lying all round the house (who says doing science can't be fun sometimes?). Then he let the owner back in. What did Nick do? He looked 'guilty', just as if he'd done the shredding himself. But he hadn't, of course. What Nick had really learned was this: 'Paper on the floor when my owner comes home means there will be crossness.' He hadn't learned what his owner wanted him to, which was 'I don't want you to shred toilet paper ever again!'

Some dogs just love to chew, so if they have to be left alone, it's a good idea to leave them with something they are allowed to gnaw on (and shut the bathroom door).

To be happy, dogs need people. Most dogs enjoy the company of other dogs, and of course it helps that they can talk to each other in dog-language. But humans are more important to them. They don't have to *see* their humans all the time, unless they're feeling really worried about something. It's usually enough for them just to pick up their owners' smell and hear them moving around the house. But for pet dogs, losing their owner would be the worst thing ever.

When Mum and Dad first adopted Rusty from the rescue centre, the people there told them how they should train him, so he would feel OK when they had to leave him on his own.

All dogs have to be left alone sometimes,

so it's best for them that they learn that this isn't the end of the world. The trick is to teach the dog to relax while the family is getting ready to leave, rather than getting stressed out. Lots of dogs feel worried whenever they hear someone picking up their car keys — because they know that may mean that everyone is going to disappear. Because dogs aren't very good at thinking about what might happen in the future, most of them can't work out that after people go out, they almost always come back quite soon. They can't stop themselves from thinking that they might have been abandoned completely, and that makes them really stressed.

The people at the rescue centre told Mum and Dad that they shouldn't leave Rusty alone

for the first couple of weeks, so he could get to know and trust them. During this time, to stop Rusty from getting anxious when they did have to all go out without him, they had to play a sort of game with him. First, they just pretended that they were going out. They had to put on their coats and pick up the car keys, and wait to see if Rusty got upset.

He did look puzzled for a moment, but as soon as he relaxed, they gave him a biscuit as a reward. Then they took off their coats and put the car keys away.

The next time they played the game, after they put their coats on they actually went towards the front door. Rusty looked sad straight away, so they put the treats away, then stopped playing the game for a few minutes. After a few times, Rusty began to forget that he didn't like them going out, and tried to work out why he wasn't getting the treats any more. He found that if he went to his bed and lay down, the treats started again.

Once they were sure that Rusty didn't mind them getting ready to go out, Mum and Dad could start actually going out of the front door for a few moments.

Rusty got treats for being on his bed just before they left, and for being calm when they came back indoors. Gradually, he felt better about being on his own, though it would never be his favourite time.

The people at the rescue centre insisted that Rusty must never be left alone until Mum and Dad were sure that this training had worked. Too often, dog owners think that dogs will be OK on their own as soon as they've got to know their new house.

But these people miss the point that dogs need their owners more than they need a place of their own.

Sometimes if a dog is badly upset when left alone, the owners will get another dog, thinking that they will be company for one another, but that usually doesn't work. A dog can tell the difference between humans and another dog, and it's human company that he will miss. In fact sometimes when the second dog sees the first dog getting upset, she may get panicky too, even before she realises why. The result: *two* dogs who wreck the house whenever their owners go out, not just *one*!

Rusty's still not one hundred per cent happy about Dad leaving him on his own, but he's taught himself how to relax while

they're out. He does get some comfort from the smell of the family around the house. Sometimes he'll snuggle up on a worn T-shirt that Ned has forgotten to pick up, and Ned's smell comforts him. But he still doesn't like being left in strange places, mainly because they smell wrong – especially boarding kennels that smell of disinfectant.

The school run

Rusty wakes up when he hears Dad's keys in the door. Rusty rushes to greet him. Lots of dogs get so excited when their families come home that they jump all over them, or even run out into the street while the front door is open. That's dangerous, because there might be a car going past. Rusty used to jump up when he was a puppy, but he doesn't now, because Dad and Mum have trained him to wait until everyone's in the house, and then everyone

will say hello to him, one at a time.

When Mum and Dad went to the rescue centre to get Rusty, they were given a lot of other advice about how best to train him. Not just how to help him keep calm while they were out, but more obvious things, like making sure he came back to them when they called his name. That's very important, because dogs that won't come back have to be kept on the lead all the time, and that's not a lot of fun for the owner. Worse, it stops the dog from doing all the sniffing around that he wants to do. So training is an essential part of having a happy dog.

Dad fetches Rusty's lead and some snacks for the kids and they head out of the door together.

There's a lamp-post at the end of their road, and naturally it's a very popular pee-post! Rusty has had a lot of fun watching all the dogs trying to out-pee each other. Big dogs cock their legs a bit so that they can pee a little way up the post. When little dogs come along and sniff where the big dogs have been, they feel a bit inferior, so they lift their leg as high as it can go, and pee as far up the post as possible without toppling over. Sometimes, while they're wobbling on three legs, their owner gets so far ahead that the lead goes tight and they have to stop peeing straight away to avoid an embarrassing topple! Some long skinny dogs have to stop so far beyond the post that they can't see what they're doing, and miss the post entirely, which makes Rusty chuckle to himself.

As Dad and Rusty get closer to Bella and Ned's school, they meet up with other parents who have also brought their dogs with them. Big dogs, little dogs, skinny dogs, dogs with a bit of a weight problem, dogs with curly tails, dogs with long straight tails, dogs with short coats, dogs with long woolly fur who can hardly see where they're going.

Dogs come in more shapes and sizes than any other animal on the planet, but Rusty has learned – mainly by sniffing them – that they are actually all dogs, just like him.

Unlike many dogs, Rusty has a proper tail and proper ears and can use those when he's talking to other dogs.

Other breeds are not so lucky. Some have very stumpy tails that won't wag properly, and won't go up or down to change the meaning of the wag.

Some have very heavy ears that hardly move at all when the dog tries to flatten them.

Some have lots of fur over their eyes which makes it difficult for them to see where they're going.

Dogs with squashed faces can have difficulty breathing, especially when they get older. They also have difficulty sniffing.

Rusty watches a pug spending ages trying to sniff a lamp-post, before her owner loses patience and drags her off down the road. Rusty is a cross-breed and should be able to live a long and healthy life, but many pure-bred dogs get sick because their parents were not healthy either. That's sad!

Sadly, because humans are obsessed with appearances, they often decide that they must have a dog that looks a particular way. These people look on the internet for someone who's selling cute puppies of the breed that they've convinced themselves that they must have. Sadly some of those come from horrible places where the puppies and their mothers are fed by machines and never get any cuddles from humans. (Some people call them 'puppy factories' because they're like factory farms.) The pups are often not very healthy either, and even when they get to live with a loving family, it's a while before they are well enough to learn that people can be kind to them. Dogs like this need special help so that they can stop feeling scared.

Scaredy dogs

On the way to school, Rusty goes up to sniff a tall skinny dog, and the tall skinny dog tries to sniff back. But as soon as Dad, a human she doesn't know, comes near, she runs and hides behind her owner's legs. Because dogs come in many shapes and sizes, it's not surprising that they have many different ways of showing that they're frightened. It's important that children like you learn all of those signs, because a scared dog can snap at you if you get too close. Dogs don't automatically know that children aren't likely to hurt them.

A dog that's starting to feel a bit nervous is not so easy to spot, because he may do things that dogs do all the time, just in a slightly weird way. So, you might see a dog licking his nose or his lips for no obvious reason, or yawning when he couldn't possibly be tired, or blinking over and over again, or panting when there's no reason for him to be hot. You should also be careful if his eyes are wide, wide open enough to show lots of white around the dark part. If he also keeps looking away, or his ears are scrunched down on to his head, then definitely don't get any closer. Some dogs will even roll over and show their bellies when they're upset, but they are NOT asking you to tickle them. And whatever you think you've spotted about the dog, tell an adult why you're concerned – lots of grown-ups don't know how to spot a nervous dog either.

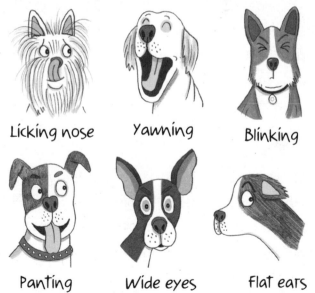

Licking nose   Yawning   Blinking

Panting   Wide eyes   Flat ears

Dad and Rusty are waiting at a crossing. It's a busy road, so Dad tells Rusty to 'sit'. Just as we do, dogs listen out for two different things when someone speaks to them. They try to work out both what the word is – 'sit' – and also how it is said. Is it 'sit' or 'SIT!'? Because humans are so important to them, they are better than any other animal at recognising what tone of voice a person is using. Is it happy talk, or sad talk, or angry talk? Often they pay more attention to the emotion in the person's voice than they do to the word itself, because they are so anxious to please us.

Dogs learn best when a good thing happens right after they've done something right. So when you're training them, you need to give them the treat at just the right moment. It goes like this: you say, 'Here, boy,' the dog runs over, you give him a biscuit. After a few times, the dog knows that when he hears 'Here, boy,' it's fun to run to the person who said it (and there might be a snack as well!). Snacks, not smacks! Not so complicated, after all.

Dad realises he's a bit early for school, so on the way, he lets Rusty have a quick run in the park. He unclips Rusty's lead and Rusty runs around sniffing. He catches a whiff of a lovely cheesy smell: a small child has a snack. He starts to go up to the child, but Dad sees the child is scared and calls out, 'Here, boy'. Rusty runs over to Dad, who rubs his head and says, 'Good boy'.

Just as Dad is putting Rusty back on his lead, they hear an owner shouting angrily at her dog while she is still coming back to her. What does that dog do? She slows down, and runs around in a bit of circle, because the shouting has confused her. Why is her owner shouting at her, when she's usually delighted when she comes back to her? Often, the reason is way beyond the understanding of a dog.

Perhaps the owner is worried that someone else in the park is going to shout at *her* for letting her dog get too close to their child/picnic/whatever. It's much more sensible to keep encouraging the dog to come back, and then when she's safely on the lead, go and apologise quietly to the person who's got upset. After all, not everyone likes dogs, and some children are more scared of dogs than perhaps they need to be.

Dogs are happiest when they know what to do and when they should do it. Training is important for dogs, but not if that means hitting the dog whenever it does something wrong, which is what some owners seem to think. Remember, dogs learn best when they get something nice for doing something right. It doesn't have to be cheese, like in the story about the scared dog in the rescue centre. 'Something nice' could mean a biscuit, or a game of chasing a ball, or it could be just a friendly pat on the head. Some people find that simply talking to their dog in a kind voice can be enough, but that doesn't seem to work for all dogs (maybe they're not as smart as Rusty!), so it's usually best to stick to treats and cuddles.

Another big mistake that owners make when they're trying to call their dogs is to think that the dog must understand everything they say, and is just choosing to ignore most of it. (Out of spite? Oh, no, because we already know that's not very likely.)

So, how much of what people say does Rusty actually understand? First of all, he can recognise lots of sounds, and knows what

action, or thing (or person) each sound refers to. He has to learn each one, just like you had to when you were very young. But dogs are not nearly as quick as children at learning words. There are a few 'genius' dogs who know the names of hundreds of objects, and will fetch each one as each word is spoken. But that's still not very clever compared to Ned and Bella. At their age, they're probably learning about ten new words *every day*, and without even noticing they're doing it. Even six year olds know about twenty thousand words, although they may only use two or three thousand when they speak. Also, Ned and Bella can understand complicated sentences, that may refer to the present, the future or the past. No dog has ever been able to do this.

Dad and Rusty get to the school gates just in time to meet Bella and Ned, who have probably learned even more words today! Rusty gives them both a good snuffle as they rub his head, just so he can remind himself how their smells change when they've been in school all day.

What dogs understand
(and what they don't get at all)

Everyone's back at home now. Ned's in the living room watching a video on Mum's tablet. Bella's doing her homework at the table. Dad's preparing dinner, and Mum's got a basket of washing in her hands. Rusty's on his bed, but he's not asleep, he's keeping a keen eye on everything that's going on.

Dogs are always trying to work out what their owners want from them, and that's why they make such wonderful friends. They don't just listen to us and watch out for what we're doing, they can easily learn a lot about us in a way that no other animal can manage.

Dogs walk on four legs and rely on their noses to tell them most of what's going on. It must be really hard for them to learn that we take very little notice of what our noses are telling us, and we have arms instead of front legs. Despite our differences, young dogs quickly learn that humans use their hands for lots of things that front paws are useless for, such as pointing at things that they want us to be interested in. Mum points to Rusty's bed when she wants him to lie down on it, and towards the back door when

it's time for him to go out in the garden.

Being able to understand what a pointing finger means is clever enough, but Rusty, like lots of other dogs, can even follow a pointing *foot*. Why would Mum want to point with her foot? That would be when she's in a hurry and can't use her hands, like now, when she is carrying a basket full of washing.

If she points with her foot when her hands are free, Rusty often ignores her, because he understands that pointing with a foot is only meant for him if the person has their hands full. That shows that dogs are really, really smart!

But there are some things that we do all the time that dogs just don't get. Forks and spoons – why bother with those when you can just stick your nose in the food? What's that noisy thing that humans push around the house picking up all the interesting smelly stuff that's got trodden in from outdoors? Why did Dad need a pointy metal thing when he was trying to put together the cupboard in the hall? Why did he get cross when he dropped it? Tools – what are they, and why are they better than teeth and paws?

Anyway, dogs don't need tools, they have humans! When Rusty needs something badly all he has to do is look at Mum or Dad and give a little bark to let them know that he's not just fooling around.

Rusty notices that his ball is stuck under the cupboard in the room where Bella is doing her homework. He could try to drag it out with his paw, but he knows that he only has to look at it and then at her and then back at the ball, and she will work out that he needs something doing.

As soon as she sees Rusty's ball, she fetches a ruler from her pencil case and hooks it out for him.

Another thing that people do, especially grown-ups, is stand in front of the shiny mirror thing on the wall in the hallway, and gaze into it as if there was something interesting in there. The first time Rusty saw his reflection in the mirror, he nearly jumped out of his skin! He thought, 'There's another dog in the house! Quick, tell Mum and Dad!' And he ran into the kitchen, barking. They just laughed.

So he went back to the mirror and the dog was still there! Bark, bark, bark! Now Bella and Ned were laughing too. The whole family was beside themselves with mirth. So Rusty went up to the mirror, and had a sniff. 'It doesn't smell like a dog, doesn't sound like a dog, so it can't be a dog. Silly me!' After that, Rusty ignored the mirror and he has never realised that *he* is the dog he sees in the mirror!

Friends and strangers

It's now the evening and Rusty is definitely ready for his dinner. But just as he thinks he hears his bowl coming out of the cupboard, the doorbell rings. It's the man from next door, and he's brought his new dog with him. She's a little fluffy white dog, and Bella especially thinks that she's extremely cute.

Rusty is not too pleased when everyone makes a huge fuss of this intruder (as he sees it). This is Rusty's house! This is Rusty's family! They tell him to sit and be quiet, but he just

can't control himself. He thinks he might like the little dog just fine once he gets to know her, but right now he's really jealous of the attention she's getting. He pushes himself between Mum and the dog, looking up at her as if to say, 'You're *my* mum, not hers!'

Mum understands, and she leaves the kids playing with the dog while she gives Rusty some one-to-one attention, and soon he calms down.

The man from next door doesn't stay long, and after he's gone, Rusty gets his dinner and then settles down on his bed. He can still smell where the little dog has been, but he's forgotten about being jealous. Dogs don't usually fret about things that have happened in the past, because they live in the here and now. If he meets the little dog tomorrow, he'll probably be delighted to have a game with her – provided the humans don't get in the way!

One of the pack

After everyone has eaten, Ned and Bella watch some TV and then go upstairs to get ready for bed, while Rusty settles down in front of the fire. Dad fancies himself as a bit of a musician, and brings one of his harmonicas downstairs to practise a tune he's heard on the radio (if you haven't seen one, a harmonica is a small rectangular instrument that you suck or blow into to make different notes). To everyone's surprise (including Rusty's!), as soon as Dad starts to play, Rusty's

ears shoot upright and he jumps out of his bed. He rushes over to Dad and sits down, staring up at the ceiling. Then he begins to howl. And howl. And howl.

Dad stops playing; Rusty stops howling, and stares at him. Dad starts again; so does Rusty. By now Mum is giggling fit to burst, and Ned and Bella have both appeared half way down the stairs, wondering what all the commotion is about. Even Dad has to stop playing because he's laughing so much.

Rusty looks around the room, wondering what all the fuss is about. He had been having such a wonderful time! Until then, he hadn't even realised that he could howl! The sound of the harmonica had stirred up a vague memory deep in his mind, something, though Rusty doesn't know it, that goes way back to his distant ancestors.

Many thousands of years ago there were no dogs anywhere in the world, but there were some especially friendly wolves, who started living with people and over many generations gradually turned into dogs. But before wolves started living with human families, they lived with their wolf families, called packs. Their food didn't come from the supermarket, they had to get it for themselves by hunting.

Just as Rusty's human family is really important to him, so these ancient wolves depended on their pack. Their pack would be made up of a mother and a father wolf with their grown-up pups, and some little ones that they kept hidden away in an underground den. It would take several years for the pups to learn how to hunt, and so they would have starved if they ever got separated from their parents. They all needed to stick together. If one ever got lost, they

would call out to the others by howling. A howl can travel through many miles of thick woodland, so it was the best way of letting the family know where you were. When they heard their pups howling, the parents would howl back, and soon everyone would be back together again. However, if the pack was out hunting and heard a howl that they didn't recognise, they'd know that there was another pack nearby, and head off in a different direction to avoid a fight.

There are a few breeds of dog, such as huskies, that still howl to each other all the time, but most dogs only howl when they're really upset and they've found that barking or whining hasn't worked. Dad's harmonica must have reminded Rusty that although he is definitely a dog, in his head he is still a tiny bit wolf, and needs to keep in touch with his pack.

Dad thinks it's a bit late for the neighbours to be disturbed by Rusty's howling, so he puts the harmonica back in his pocket. He's puzzled that Rusty reacted the way he did, though, and thinks he'll get his harmonica out again another day to see if Rusty will howl again (he will!).

Now it's bedtime for Mum and Dad, and Rusty settles down for the night. He doesn't

mind that he's downstairs and the family are all upstairs. He can still smell each one of them from the tiny scraps of scent that they have, without knowing it, left behind during the day, and that comforts him.

Good night, Rusty!

Happy dogs

Rusty doesn't understand that people don't know about the World of Smells, but you do, now! And now you understand that dogs and children learn about the world in slightly different ways, and how happy dogs feel when they're part of a human family. And you also understand more about what dogs are trying to tell us by the way they move, and how they wag their tails.

Dogs can teach us a lot. They can help us understand what it's like to be an animal, and

how important animals are in our lives. And a world without animals would be a very sad place.

The way that dogs see the world isn't a secret. You can tell anyone you like, and especially other children who have dogs at home. It's good for dogs when people understand them, because then everyone gets along so much better. Happy dogs make people happy!

ACKNOWLEDGEMENTS

A big thank-you to all the humans who helped me with this book, especially Beatrice Bradshaw, Melanie Pressey, Senan Bestic, Sam Bradshaw, Amy Ledger, Clare Elsom for bringing Rusty to life, Professor David Hopkins, Allison DeFrees, John Ash, Patrick Walsh, Chloe Sackur and Eloise Wilson.

Author Questions & Answers

Hello John!

You're an anthrozoologist - what a long title! - what does it mean?

An anthrozoologist is someone who studies how people and animals get on together. Some anthrozoologists are interested in how animals make people happy (or sad), or how our ancestors treated their animals (often, not as well as we do!) but I'm most interested in what our animals are trying to tell us, if only we understood them better.

What made you decide to become an anthrozoologist?

I'm a biologist, and most biologists study wild animals (and plants). But I think that the pet animals that live in our houses are just as interesting, so I decided to study them instead.

What's the most exciting thing you discovered when studying dogs?

I think the most important thing I've discovered is how much dogs miss us when they're left alone. That was exciting in a way, because it shows how much our dogs love us, but also sad, because we found that millions of dogs get unhappy every day when their owners go out. Dogs can be trained to cope when they're on their own. It would be so good if more owners knew that.

What are the four most important things to consider before getting a dog?

1. Are you going to be able to look after your dog for the next ten or fifteen years? Which might mean, who is going to look after your dog when you've grown up and left home?

2. Can your family afford a dog? They cost between £50 and £80 a month to look after, and much more if they get seriously ill.

3. Choose your dog carefully. Don't be misled by cute pictures or videos. Do you really want a puppy that's going to turn your life upside-down for months? There are always lots of well-behaved grown-up dogs waiting to be adopted from shelters. If you do decide to get a puppy from a breeder, make sure you see the puppy with its mother. Puppies bought on the internet have often not been looked after properly.

4. Check the advice on the RSPCA and PDSA websites in the UK, or the animal welfare websites for your country.

What are the three most important things to remember when looking after a pet dog?

Dogs are not born knowing how to behave around people, they have to be taught. The three most important things about training are:

1. Get expert advice from a trainer who uses rewards to train dogs. It's easy to find this in books or on the internet. Train your dog to come to you when you are out for a walk. No-one likes a dog that bounces up at them, and a dog that is out of control can run across a road and get hit by a car.

2. If you have a puppy, it will need to learn about the world, or it will grow up to be timid or aggressive. This learning is known as 'socialisation'. Gradually introduce your puppy to all the things and kinds of people that it will meet when it gets older. Washing machines, hoovers, traffic, postmen, crowds of people are just a few. There's lots of advice on this on the internet.

3. Teach your dog how not to feel abandoned when you go out. A hundred years ago, this wasn't a problem as dogs were allowed everywhere. Nowadays we may have to leave them at home, but they hate it. Search #DogKind for how to do it.

Did you have a pet dog when you were growing up?

My dad was often away at sea, so we couldn't have a dog when I was a child. I adopted my first dog Alexis when I was at uni. He was a cross between a black Labrador and a Jack Russell terrier, and a few years later he was joined by Ivan, a cross between a black Labrador and an Airedale terrier!

Was Rusty based on a real dog?

Rusty is a mixture between Alexis, my first dog, and Ginger, my mother's first dog. He was a Cairn terrier, and although I never met him, I feel I know a lot about him from the many stories she told me.

If you were a dog and had a dog's sense of smell, what would your favourite smell be? What would your worst smell be?

Best smells: food, and my owner (some dogs that hate being left alone can be calmed down by leaving your grubby T-shirt next to their bed).

Worst: disinfectant. Reminds me of kennels.

If you had a superpower that allowed you to talk to dogs, what would you ask your pet dog?

'Do you know what "tomorrow" means?' Dogs don't seem to plan for the future, but I'd love to know for sure.

As well as being an anthrozoologist, you are also a writer. What made you decide to write a book for children?

The idea of getting a dog often comes from the children rather than their mum or dad. I'd like them to understand better what they're asking for, and even be able to tell their parents how to do it right!

What advice would you give to anyone who's thinking about becoming a writer?

Think of something that fascinates you, and find out as much as you can about it. Become an expert. If you do that properly, the actual writing should be easy.

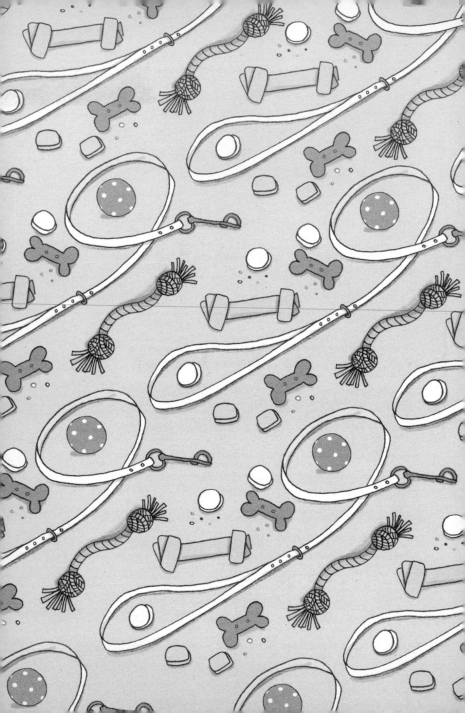